THE CORSICAN HIGH LEVEL ROUTE

Front Cover: The Spasimata Valley
Back Cover: Brêche de Capitello

THE CORSICAN HIGH LEVEL ROUTE

THE CORSICAN HIGH LEVEL ROUTE

Walking the GR20

by
ALAN CASTLE

CICERONE PRESS
MILNTHORPE, CUMBRIA, ENGLAND.

© *Alan Castle 1987*
ISBN 1 85284 100 1
First Published 1987
New Edition 1992

British Library Cataloguing-in-Publication Data. A catalogue record for this book is available from the British Library.

For Bebs, who came too.

LA VRAIE LIBERTÉ C'EST LE VAGABONDAGE
J.J.ROUSSEAU (1712-78)

ACKNOWLEDGEMENTS

The author would like to thank his wife Beryl Castle, for all the encouragement given during the writing of this guidebook, and also his French mother-in-law (Andrée Cain) for helping to unravel the complexities of the French language. Grateful thanks also go to Joan Newman for her careful typing of the manuscript. **Photos by the author except where stated otherwise. Photos on colour pages by Maurice Tedd.**

CONTENTS

INTRODUCTION

Corsica 7
GR20 7
When to go 8
Travelling to Corsica 9
Travelling on Corsica 10
Le Parc Naturel Régional de la Corse 10
Equipment 11
Food Provisions 11
Water 12
Mountain Huts 12
Camping/Bivouacking 13
Litter 13
Fire 13
Wildlife 14
Insurance 14
Language 14
Training 14
Special Problems 15
Maps 15
How to walk the GR20. Variations on a theme 15
How to use the guide 17
Summary table of the GR20 19

GUIDE

DAY 1	Calenzana to Spasimata 20
DAY 2	Spasimata to Altore 25
DAY 3	Altore to Mori 30
DAY 4	Mori to Manganu 37
DAY 5	Manganu to Pietra-Piana 41
DAY 6	Pietra-Piana to L'Onda 47
DAY 7	L'Onda to Vizzavona 51
DAY 8	Vizzavona to Capanelle 56
DAY 9	Capanelle to Col de Verde 59

Continued overleaf

DAY 10	Col de Verde to D'Usciolu	61
DAY 11	D'Usciolu to D'Asinao	65
DAY 12	D'Asinao to Paliri	69
DAY 13	Paliri to Conca	74

APPENDICES

APPENDIX 1	Mountain Huts on the GR20	79
APPENDIX 2	Facilities on the GR20	82
APPENDIX 3	Bibliography	85
APPENDIX 4	Useful Addresses	86

Advice to Readers

Readers are advised that whilst every effort is taken by the author to ensure the accuracy of this guidebook, changes can occur which may affect the contents. It is advisable to check locally on transport, accommodation, shops etc but even rights-of-way can be altered and, more especially overseas, paths can be eradicated by landslip, forest fires or changes of ownership.

The publisher would welcome notes of any such changes

INTRODUCTION

Corsica
Corsica (in French, Corse) is a mountainous island in the Mediterranean some 50 miles (81km) from the continent of Europe. It has an approximate length from north to south of 110 miles (177km) and a width from east to west of about 50 miles (81km). It is a department of France and its capital is Ajaccio on the western seaboard. The major commercial port is Bastia in the north.

The interior is mainly mountainous in character and is sparsely populated. There are a few isolated settlements in the valleys and several mountain farms (bergeries) are to be found, but many of these are only occupied during the summer months. The Vizzavona Pass in the centre of the island takes both road and rail, and roughly divides the mountain massifs into two areas. In the north is Haute Corse where the highest summits (Monte Cinto 8,887ft-2,706m, Monte Rotondo 8,611ft-2,622m and Monte d'Oro 7,846ft-2,389m) are to be found. In the south (Corse de Sud) the scale of the mountains is a little less grand and here the principal peaks are Monte Renoso (7,731ft-2,354m) and Incudine (7,008ft-2,134m). On the west coast the mountains reach almost to the coast, but on the east side of the island are wide fertile plains stretching to the sea. The coastal scenery is some of the best in Europe.

The summer temperatures on the coast average 20-25°C, but temperatures in excess of 30°C frequently occur. Temperatures are obviously somewhat lower in the mountains. The total rainfall during the summer is fairly small but violent thunderstorms are not uncommon. Snowfall is usually quite heavy during the winter and snow often persists in the mountains into the late spring.

GR20
The GR20 is one of a number of official long distance footpaths in France. The GR (Grande Randonnée) network of footpaths is very extensive, some 24,800 miles (40,000km) of path having been described and waymarked. Each GR route has been allotted a number. The GR20 is the principal official long distance footpath in Corsica and it is generally considered to be the most difficult of all

the GR routes. It is extremely popular and in the main summer months many hundreds of walkers (mainly French and German) are to be found along the way.

The GR20 runs from Calenzana in the north-west of the island across the mountains of Haute Corse to Vizzavona and from there it traverses the mountains of southern Corsica to finish at the village of Conca, near to Porto Vecchio in the south-east. The trail is well waymarked throughout with red and white flashes on rocks, boulders and trees. The route is wholly mountainous and for nearly all of its length is above the 3,000 feet (914m) contour line. The highest point reached on the GR20 is on the Col de la Haute Route (7,245ft-2,206m) in Haute Corse. The total amount of ascent (and descent) is some 32,000 feet (9,744m). All of the 110 miles (177km) of the trail lie within the Parc Naturel Régional de la Corse. The crux of the GR20 is a traverse of the Cirque de la Solitude in the northern part of the island. This very imposing granite cirque is crossed with the aid of considerable lengths of fixed rope and metal cable. The route is a complete traverse of the Corsican mountains and is scenically of the highest order. It is a serious undertaking requiring previous backpacking and mountain scrambling experience. Truly one of the classic walks in Europe.

When to go
Despite their Mediterranean location, the mountains of Corsica carry snow for much of the year. You can expect to find snow on the high passes even into June. The months of July and August tend to be very hot and heat haze often obscures the views, but this is the season during which the majority of walkers tackle the GR20. September and even October can provide good conditions, although the risk of weather deterioration is greater. It would be unwise to set out after mid-October as heavy snowfall is not unusual from that time onwards. The optimum time for the walk might be the first two weeks in September. At this period the number of walkers on the route is likely to be less than in July and August, and hence the huts will be far less crowded. Moreover, it is less likely to be as fiercely hot as in the height of the summer, but should, nevertheless, be before the autumn deterioration of the weather has occurred.

Travelling to Corsica

The most practical method of travelling to Corsica for anyone living in Great Britain is by air. The flight time is about two hours. Daily flights operate to Ajaccio airport and it is also possible to fly to Calvi (the latter being very close to the start of the GR20). Most flights depart from Gatwick or Heathrow, but there are sometimes departures from certain other airports in this country, eg. Manchester and Glasgow. Low-fare (APEX and similar) flights can be booked, and these operate usually about four days a week. Many of the above flights are not direct, but are via Paris or Nice. There are many charter flights to Corsica. These are cheap and are direct to the island, but if travelling in the main season it is important to book well in advance. One of the main tour operators in Britain is Falcon Holidays.

For those with more time available it is possible to go by ferry to the continent, travel by train or coach to one of the Mediterranean seaports, and from there take a ferry to Corsica. This would require about two days of travel and is unlikely to be much cheaper than a charter flight to the island. The main advantage of this method of travel is that you will probably not be restricted by a fixed return date, as will be the case with most flights.

The main ferry services are as follows:

1) Marseille - Ajaccio. Up to three sailings per week with extra sailings in high season. Twelve hours duration.
2) Marseille - Bastia. Two sailings per week during the summer. Twelve hours duration.
3) Nice - Ajaccio. Four sailings per week in high season. Seven hours duration.
4) Nice - Bastia. Three sailings per week in high season. Seven hours duration.
5) Nice - Calvi. Three sailings per week in July and three sailings per week in August. Six hours duration.
6) La Spezia (Italy) - Bastia. Daily from June 20 to September 30.
7) Livorno (Italy) - Bastia. Daily from June 2 to September 23. Three days a week from April 7 to June 1 and September 24 to October 14. Four hours duration.
8) Piombino (Italy) - Bastia. As for Livorno - Bastia. Three hours duration.

Travelling on Corsica

Trains: There is an excellent mountain train that links Ajaccio to Calvi and to Bastia. This mountain railway, built in the 1880s, is a considerable feat of engineering and penetrates the heart of the island. The fare is relatively inexpensive and a trip on this railway is highly recommended. It is very useful for those walking the GR20 as one of the stations is at Vizzavona, the half-way stage of the trail. Furthermore, it terminates at Calvi, which is near to the start of the walk. The trains run throughout the year, the somewhat inferior winter timetable usually beginning during the latter part of September. There are normally at least two trains daily in both directions. The journey time from Ajaccio to Calvi is about five hours. The line divides at Porto Leccia and from here one can travel to Bastia.

Buses: There is not an extensive network of buses on the island, but the major towns are connected by bus. The most important routes for those walking the GR20 are the following:- 1. Ajaccio to Calvi. Journey time about ten hours (the train is much faster and more scenic). 2. Porto Vecchio to Ajaccio. Journey time about four hours. Other bus routes include Ajaccio-Corte-Bastia and Porto Vecchio-Bastia. There is no bus service from Conca. The nearest bus from the end of the GR20 is at Sainte-Lucie de Porto-Vecchio about 3.5 miles (5.6km) from Conca. This bus service goes to Porto Vecchio or to Bastia. There is a local bus from Calvi to Calenzana but it operates only during the summer months (the last service of the year is usually in mid-September). Note that these services only run once or sometimes twice a day during the summer months. Outside the main tourist season the buses are more restricted. Further information can be obtained by contacting the Tourist Office in Corsica (see Appendix 4).

Taxis: These are fairly expensive on Corsica. They can be hired from several centres in the vicinity of the GR20 eg. Bonifato, Guagno, Zicavo, Zonza, Quenza and Conca.

Le Parc Naturel Régional de la Corse

The mountain areas of Corsica are controlled by the 'Parc Naturel Régional de la Corse' (PNR). This body was established in 1972 and the entire GR20 is within its boundaries. Assisted by a large number of park wardens, the function of the PNR is to preserve the interior's outstanding beauty. Among other things, the wardens construct and maintain the mountain huts, build suspension bridges (passerelles) over the more difficult river crossings, look after the general upkeep of the mountain trails, protect the flora and fauna of the island and control forestry activities.

Equipment

Anyone contemplating this walk should be sufficiently experienced to know the basic backpacking equipment that will be required and so this will not be overstressed here. There is obviously a need to keep the weight carried as low as possible.

Although the GR20 can be walked using hut and other accommodation only, it is advisable to take a small tent, or at least a bivvy-bag for emergency bivouacking, or in case the huts are overcrowded. A sleeping-bag is also required, as blankets are not usually supplied in the mountain huts. A lightweight bag will suffice.

If at any time you are forced to camp away from a mountain hut, then you will need your own stove and fuel. Remember that gas canisters, petrol or methylated spirits cannot be carried on board an aircraft, and so these will have to be purchased when you arrive in Corsica.

Specialist equipment should not be required, although some parties may wish to carry a rope in case of difficulties. An ice-axe should not be necessary, unless the mountaineer is going out of the summer season.

For much of the time, shorts and a tee-shirt will probably be found the most comfortable attire, although warmer clothes must be carried in case the weather deteriorates, and for the evenings. A sun hat is strongly recommended, as is barrier cream to prevent sunburn. Good boots are essential and waterproof clothing must be carried.

Food Provisions

Food is probably the most important item to be carried. If you do not intend to deviate from the route to replenish your food supply, then it is essential that you carry enough food to last for at least six days.

This will probably mean that the basis of your rations will have to be dehydrated meals. These are best bought at home as they are not easily obtained in Corsica. They are also much cheaper in Britain and a good variety is available. The main places for restocking on the route are at Vizzavona (Day 7), and at Capenelle (Day 8) and at the Col de la Bavella (Day 12). Where food can be purchased by making a detour from the GR20, then this is indicated in the route description, but remember that these deviations can be very time-consuming and tiring, and may not even result in getting the food that you require. For further details see Appendix 2.

Water

Lack of water on the GR20 could prove a problem. It is *essential* to carry sufficient water whilst in the Corsican mountains, as heat exhaustion and dehydration can rapidly develop when carrying heavy loads on steep mountainsides in the heat of the day. These can be fatal. Make sure you bring enough water carriers with you. Wherever there are likely to be long stages between water sources, then this is mentioned in the route description.

Mountain Huts

There is an excellent system of mountain huts (refuges) spaced at approximately one-day walking intervals along the GR20. These are usually built of wood and stone and most are controlled by the PNR. They provide simple accommodation and usually consist of a 'unisex' dormitory with bunks and mattresses and a kitchen/living room. There are usually calor gas stoves provided and a small collection of utensils (pots and pans, plates, dishes, knives, forks and spoons).

There is normally a warden in residence throughout the summer months and he or she will collect the overnight fee. There is a flat rate system for all the huts and they are relatively inexpensive. There is no reduction in charge for members of any of the alpine clubs and there is no booking system. Sleeping places are allocated on a first-come, first-served basis.

No meals of any kind are provided at these refuges and the wardens only stock provision for their own use. The huts do not have generators, but usually have some form of portable calor gas lighting and a supply of candles. Several of the huts are equipped with solar panels. It is useful to carry a torch for use in the huts at night and in the early morning.

For details on the individual huts see Appendix 1.

Camping/Bivouacking

The PNR authorities do not allow wild camping along the GR20 under normal circumstances. This rule, which is rigorously enforced, has been introduced because of the litter problem on the island and also of the great risk of fire. However, it is possible to camp in the vicinity of the mountain huts (usually for a nominal fee) and at some of them a fenced-off area is provided for this purpose. Unless you are camped in such a compound you are strongly advised not to leave a camp unattended at any time, as it is very likely to be raided by the numerous semi-wild pigs that are found all over the mountain areas. These will eat or destroy your food and do considerable damage to your belongings.

During the summer months it rarely becomes very cold at nights, even in the mountains, and sleeping out under the stars can be a pleasant experience.

Litter

Unfortunately you will find considerable quantities of litter in the Corsican mountains. Do not add to this problem. If you are prepared to carry large quantities of food across miles of near wilderness, then you must be prepared to carry out the packaging in which it arrived.

Fire

With its Mediterranean climate, maquis and forest-covered mountainsides it is perhaps inevitable that Corsica has had more than its fair share of forest fires. There have been several holocausts in recent years (1982 and 1985 in particular) when much of the island's vegetation and wildlife were destroyed. Several walkers have died in these fires. It is illegal to burn open fires in the Park and extreme caution should be exercised when using gas or liquid fuel stoves.

Wildlife

Corsica has wild sheep, goats, foxes and deer. Semi-wild pigs will be found all over the mountain regions even up to an altitude of 2,000 metres (6,568ft). Bears and wolves no longer inhabit Corsica. There are several varieties of lizard and some species of snake (these are said to be non-poisonous). At least two species of poisonous spider still survive and venomous ants can be found. Midges and mosquitoes are frequent pests during the summer months, up to 2,000 metres (6,568ft).

About one-fifth of the island is covered in forest and a dense thicket or maquis. The forests are of both pine and deciduous trees. The maquis consists of a number of scrubs and is generally tough, wiry and sharp to the touch. It presents no problems on the GR20 and the other main trails on the island, but elsewhere it can produce considerable problems of access.

Insurance

It is advisable to take out travel and medical insurance for the duration of your holiday. Ensure that your policy includes hill walking and scrambling.

Language

Corsica has been part of France for over 200 years and the official language is French, and virtually all the islanders speak this language. Nevertheless you will find the native language (Corsican) spoken occasionally, particularly in the more remote areas. Corsican has greater similarities with Italian than with French. In addition there are usually many German walkers on the GR20 many of whom speak fluent English.

Training

It is obviously advisable to arrive on the island in good physical condition. Mountain walkers who frequently visit the hills of Britain should experience no great problems, although it would be advisable to get in a few short backpacking trips to become accustomed to carrying a load.

Special Problems

The walker may encounter a number of difficulties not normally found on walks such as the Pennine Way and these are summarised here. Several of them have been discussed in more detail on previous pages. Firstly there is the problem of food provisioning along the way, and the need to carry several days' food supply when setting out. There can also be serious risk of heat exhaustion, dehydration and sunstroke and it is necessary to carry adequate quantities of water at all times. Violent thunderstorms are common on these mountains and in such circumstances exposed granite ridges are very dangerous places. There are also dangers from stonefall and from forest fires. Lastly the route requires some scrambling ability, mostly of an easy standard, but the walker will be hindered by a heavy backpack. Most of these problems can be overcome by careful planning and common sense. However, it must be emphasised that the GR20 is only suitable for those with mountain walking *and* scrambling experience and should not be undertaken lightly.

Maps

1. Didier and Richard 1:50,000
   Number 20 Corse Nord
   Number 23 Corse Sud
   The route of the GR20 is marked on these maps. These two sheets cover the entire route and are highly recommended.
2. IGN Carte Touristique 1:100,000
   Number 73 Corse Nord
   Number 74 Corse Sud
   These two maps cover the whole of the island and the route of the GR20 is marked on them.
3. IGN also publish 1:50,000 and 1:25,000 maps of Corsica, but several sheets are required to cover the whole route. IGN *(Institut Géographique National)* is the French equivalent of our own Ordnance Survey.

How to walk the GR20. Variations on a theme

There are five main ways in which the GR20 can be used as a walking holiday.

1. Walking the entire route from north to south or from south to north. The majority of backpackers walk from Calenzana to Conca and this is the direction described in this guide. Walking from north to south has the advantage of taking the more difficult sections in the first half of the walk rather than leaving them until later when the walker may be more tired. Moreover, if bad weather prevents completion of the route, then at least the more spectacular first half will not be missed. The only disadvantage of walking from north to south is that one is facing the sun for much of the day, but during the summer months the sun is fairly high in the sky for many hours, and so this is not too much of a problem. The average walker will probably require 13/14 days of good weather to complete the GR20. This must be taken into account when making travel arrangements to the island. It should be possible to fit it into a fortnight's holiday, but if time is lost due to bad weather or the need to leave the route to buy additional food, then two weeks may not be sufficient. A compromise may be to take a three-week holiday and spend the remaining time sightseeing on the island or relaxing on the numerous good beaches.

2. If the walker has limited time available but enjoys scrambling and wishes to see the best of the Corsican mountain scenery, then the Haute Corse section from Calenzana to Vizzavona is recommended. Calenzana is only 7.5 miles (12km) from a train station (Calvi) and Vizzavona is on the railway line, and so access to this area is very good.

3. If the backpacker is unsure of his/her ability to cope with the difficulties of scrambling over exposed rock whilst carrying heavy loads, but nevertheless wishes to sample the magnificent scenery of the Corsican mountains, then the southern section from Vizzavona to Conca is thoroughly recommended. Even this is not an easy undertaking and there is a considerable amount of climbing involved. Nevertheless there are few of the difficulties experienced in the northern section and moreover the route is often close to civilisation (eg. at the Col de Verde and Col de Bavella and in the numerous small villages down in the valleys a few hours off the route).

4. It is possible to spend a few days at several mountain huts on the GR20 and use these as bases to explore part of the GR20 and the

surrounding mountains. Judicious use of the available public transport would allow several sections of the GR20 to be explored in this way, without the necessity of carrying excessive loads.

5. A truly classic trip would be to walk the route in its entirety, but to take various days off to climb the peaks that are within reach of the GR20. The main possibilities are as follows:
- (i) Monte Cinto (8,887ft-2,706m) the highest peak on Corsica, from Haut Asco (Altore).
- (ii) Paglia Orba (8,292ft-2,525m) from the Mori Refuge.
- (iii) Monte Rotondo (8,611ft-2,622m) from the Refuge de Pietra-Piana.
- (iv) Monte D'Oro (7,846ft-2,389m) from the Crête de Muratello above Refuge de L'Onda.
- (v) Monte Renoso (7,731ft-2,354m) from Refuge de Capanelle.

This would be a serious expedition requiring about three weeks to complete all the summits and the GR20. It should only be attempted by experienced mountaineers, as some of the ascents require considerable scrambling and navigational ability. In particular Paglia Orba is technically a fairly difficult climb. Details of the ascents can be found in Collomb's Guide to the Corsican Mountains (see Bibliography).

How to use the Guide

The guide to the GR20 is described in 13 sections. The average party would probably complete one section per day. Some days are longer than others, the criterion being to end each night at a mountain hut or other suitable accommdation. A very fit party could finish the trail in 9-10 days, whereas a more leisurely trip would take some 15-16 days. For this reason the approximate times and distances between all the huts on the GR20 have been included in Appendix 1. Allowance must always be given for the prevailing weather conditions.

To give an overview of the day's walking, the nature of each section and the amount of ascent and descent is given at the beginning of each 'Day'. A simple grading system has been adopted for the same reason. The sections are graded from A to D.

A.   Easy walking on a well-defined path with relatively little ascent or descent and no steep climbing.

B.   Mountain walking not always on a clear path and involving considerable amounts of ascent and descent. The paths are often steep, but use of the hands is not generally necessary.

C.   Mountain walking which involves a considerable amount of scrambling over rock. The scrambling is generally of an easy standard.

D.   Scrambling over steep and exposed rock, but having the aid of fixed ropes, chains and cables.

Distances and altitudes are given in miles and feet respectively, because most English-speaking people are more familiar with this system, and also in kilometres and metres, because this is how they appear on the maps. Times are given as well as distances between the various stages. These times are those that it is considered the 'average' rambler would maintain, but no allowance is made for stopping. The time taken will obviously vary from party to party and on the prevalent conditions, but it is often useful to have an indication of the time generally required to walk a particular section. This is particularly true in the very rugged terrain of the Corsican mountains. It is a system widely used in Continental Europe.

SUMMARY TABLE OF THE GR20

STAGE		DISTANCE		ASCENT		DESCENT		ESTIMATED TIME
		miles	km	ft	m	ft	m	hrs
1.	CALENZANA - SPASIMATA							
	(ORIGINAL ROUTE)	10.1	16.2	5,097	1,552	2,092	637	7hrs 10mins
	(NEW ROUTE)	11.2	18.0	9,196	2,800	6,240	1,900	14 hrs
2.	SPASIMATA - ALTORE	6.4	10.3	3,672	1,118	1,025	312	6hrs
3.	ALTORE - MORI	6.7	10.8	3,396	1,034	3,396	1,034	7hrs 30mins
4.	MORI - MANGANU	14.5	23.4	2,095	638	3,402	1,036	8hrs
5.	MANGANU - PIETRA-PIANA	6.0	9.7	2,762	841	1,967	599	6hrs
6.	PIETRA-PIANA - L'ONDA	6.5	10.4	1,642	500	2,995	912	4hrs 30mins
7.	L'ONDA - VIZZAVONA	6.3	10.1	2,082	634	3,757	1,144	5hrs 45mins
8.	VIZZAVONA - CAPANELLE	8.6	13.7	2,782	847	614	187	4hrs 30mins
9.	CAPENELLE - COL DE VERDE	7.3	11.8	923	281	1,911	582	4hrs
10.	COL DE VERDE - D'USCIOLU	9.9	15.9	3,796	1,156	2,282	695	7hrs 30mins
11.	D'USCIOLU - D'ASINAO	10.4	16.8	2,581	786	3,304	1,006	8hrs
12.	D'ASINAO - PALIRI	9.3	15.0	1,146	349	2,591	789	5hrs 30mins
13.	PALIRI - CONCA	7.3	11.8	565	172	3,284	1,000	4hrs 30mins
TOTALS		**109.3**	**175.9**	**32,539**	**9,908**	**32,620**	**9,933**	**78hrs 55mins**
TOTALS (including new route, Day 1)		**110.4**	**177.7**	**36,638**	**11,156**	**36,768**	**11,196**	**85hrs 45mins**

Bar/Restaurant at Calenzana

DAY 1

CALENZANA to SPASIMATA

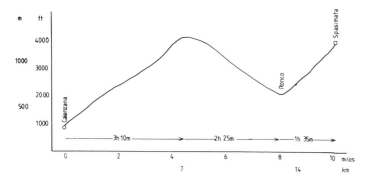

DAY 1: CALENZANA TO SPASIMATA
Original Route

Original route:	DISTANCE:	10.1 miles (16.?km)
New route:		11.2miles (18.0km)
Original route:	ASCENT:	5,097ft (1,552m)
New route:		9,196ft (2,800m)
Original route:	DESCENT:	2,092ft (637m)
New route:		6,240ft (1,900m)
Original route:	TIME:	7hrs 10mins
New route:		14hrs
Original route:	GRADE:	B
New route:		C+

Until the late 1980s the first section of the GR20 from Calenzana to Spasimata provided a fairly gentle introduction to mountain walking on the island. The first day's walk was mainly an ascent through the foothills of the north-western corner of Corsica leaving the coast and civilisation behind and heading towards the granite ridges of the island's interior. Although the climbing was fairly steep in places there was no scrambling and the day formed a fine warm-up to the greater rigours to come. However, the route passed through a forested region which was devastated by fire in the summer of 1982 and again a few years later. For this reason the authorities decided to re-route the initial stages of the GR20, avoiding the area of forest and taking the high level ridge east of the original route. In so doing they have converted a relatively easy mountain walk, easily accomplished in one day, into a more sporting high-level way along the crest. There is a new refuge servicing this route and Day 1 is now best split into two days.

The original route has not been re-waymarked and is therefore nowadays little used. However, it is still possible to follow this trail, although it is now somewhat overgrown with maquis. For those short of time, or wanting a more gentle introduction to the walk, this route is still feasible. There are splendid views from the route of the surrounding sun-baked hillsides and out to the coast at the Gulf of Calvi.

Both the original route and the new trail are described below. Note that the old route is not depicted on maps after 1986 and the new refuge of L'Ortu di u Piobbu is not indicated on maps prior to that date.

Original Route

The original trail headed south from Calenzana, climbed to a high point of about 4,000ft (1,200m) before descending to a road and river at Ronco. The hotel, restaurant and campsite at Bonifato is a short distance from here and, if time is very short on the first day, this could provide an alternative starting point for the walk (also see the 'variant' under the new route).

The GR20 starts from the church in the centre of the town. Follow the red and white markers through the narrow streets to the south-eastern edge of town. From here follow the clearly defined mule

DAY 1: CALENZANA TO SPASIMATA

track climbing up into the surrounding hills. The path soon goes through an area of forest that was largely destroyed by a devastating fire in the summer of 1982. You will pass a plaque on the left-hand side of the way, which records the death of four GR20 walkers who were trapped in the inferno in August 1982. As yet there is little shade to be found on these sun-baked hillsides. This first ascent on the GR20 is a climb of 3,225ft (982m) over a distance of 4.5 miles (7.3km). During the climb two small water sources are passed. At the summit of the path is a plateau with a superb panorama over the hills and out to the distant coast. At first the descent is gentle but this soon steepens to pass through maquis and forest to drop quite steeply down to the River Melaghia. A little before this a sign will be reached indicating the GR20 route to Spasimata to the left and a camping site at the Auberge de la Forêt to the right. Follow the GR20 route to cross the river and continue down a forest track along the left bank of the river until it merges with a second river at an area called Ronco. Immediately after the bridge here leave the forest track (which continues to the hotel Bonifato) and begin a steep ascent through forest on the left bank of the River Ficarella. After some time the river is crossed close to a dismantled suspension bridge. This crossing is over large boulders and slabs and should present no problems. Once over the river follow the path on the opposite bank. Make sure that you do not go wrong at this point by following a cairned path which leads away from the river. If you start to scramble then you have gone astray. The path to Spasimata, although steep, does not require the use of hands. The path continues to climb until a small old cabin is reached (now used as a waste storage area for the new hut). The Spasimata Refuge is found a short distance above this old cabin.

New Route

This is waymarked throughout with fresh red/white GR paint flashes. From the original route a steep ascent leads to the crest at the Bocca u Saltu. Thence a passage of several crag bands on the northern side of Capu Ghiovu leads to another col and in the next combe the Refuge L'Ortu di u Piobbu (about 8 hours). This is a new hut erected in the late 1980s.

From this refuge a steep climb is made to rejoin the crest which is traversed past the Col d'Avartoli and the Col de l'Inominata whence a steep descent leads to the Spasimata Refuge where the original route is regained. The hut at Spasimata, opened in 1984, is located in a most impressive mountain setting, with high crags all round. The walking time between the Ortu and Spasimata refuges is about 6 hours. There is some water between the two huts (the path passes a piped source before regaining the crest) although as always it is best to carry adequate quanties of water.

The new trail between Calenzana and Spasimata adds several thousand feet of extra ascent/descent to the route and the standard is mainly Grade C/D.

Note that there is a variant to the trail. At the Carrefour des Sentiers (1^{1}/$_{2}$ hours out of Calenzana) a path waymarked with orange paint stripes takes a lower route to join the original path at Ronco. This variant is feasible in a long day.

Monte Cinto, Haut d'Asco. Photo D.Unsworth

DAY 2

SPASIMATA to ALTORE

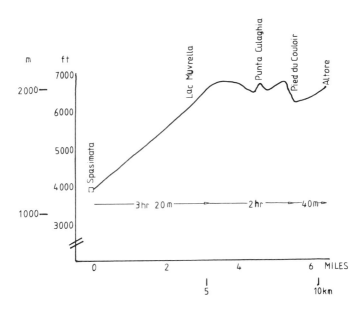

DAY 2: SPASIMATA TO ALTORE

DISTANCE: 6.4 miles (10.3km)
ASCENT: 3,672ft (1,118m)
DESCENT: 1,025ft (312m)
TIME: 6hrs
GRADE: Mainly C (short sections of D)

This is a short day in terms of both distance and time, but provides plenty of scrambling. Over short sections where there are some technical difficulties, chains or cables have been fixed to the rocks. After crossing a precarious suspension bridge, the route at first climbs to the right of the river over large slabs and boulders. Particular care is required here, especially in wet weather when these rocks become very greasy. Some of these slabs are quite

A'Muvrella and Punta Culaghia from Refuge d'Altore.
Photo: D.Unsworth

exposed and a fall here could possibly send you sliding down the rocks into the river below. After leaving the river, the route climbs an arête making use of metal cables and proceeds upwards over rocks and boulders, passing to the right of the small Lac Muvrella to reach an airy brêche. A short variation to the standard route is possible in this area to ascend to Muvrella peak, a fine viewpoint, but recommended only in good weather. The GR20 now follows the summit ridge for some way until making a very steep descent down a gully to the high valley of Asco. From here a steady ascent brings one to the site of the Refuge d'Altore. The Altore hut was burnt down in the summer of 1985 and there are no plans to re-build. There are a number of hard, earthy campsites available below the giant rock piles on which the hut was built. There is a plentiful water source in the vicinity.

Alternatively, it is possible to stay the night at the nearby hotel of Haut Asco, although this is only open in high season (July and August). This would form an excellent base for a 'day-off' to climb Monte Cinto, at 8,887ft (2,706m) the highest mountain in Corsica.

The 'tourist' ascent of this mountain from Haut Asco is described in Collomb's guide to the mountains of Corsica (see Appendix 3).

Today's route is amongst spectacular scenery but should only be attempted in good weather. It would be possible for a very fit party to continue to the new refuge at Bergerie de Ballone (see Day 3). However, bear in mind that this would add a further 4½ hours of walking/scrambling and would necessitate a crossing of the difficult Cirque de la Solitude in the late afternoon when one would probably be already quite tired. It is better to rest at Altore or Haut Asco and savour the delights (!) of the Cirque the next morning.

Route

Leave Spasimata hut and follow the waymarks to descend to the suspension bridge across the river. Cross this shaky structure and follow the route up the opposite bank of the river, over numerous slabs and boulders. Higher up the route climbs a fairly steep arête. Follow the red and white marks and a series of small cairns and make use of the fixed metal cables. Skirt to the right of the tiny Lac de Muvrella. This is polluted and water should not be taken from this area.

An alternative route can be taken from here to climb to the summit of Muvrella. This excellent viewpoint is attained by following a route marked with double yellow lines, but is only worthwhile in clear conditions. From the summit continue to follow the double yellow markers to rejoin the GR20 further along the ridge.

To follow the standard GR20 route follow the red and white flashes over rocks, slabs and boulders to reach the brêche at 6,568ft (2,000m). From this point a rough, rocky path is followed along a spectacular ridge. After a while a path leads off left (east) to Haut Asco. If you are staying the night at the hotel you should follow this path. Those not wanting Haut Asco have the option of continuing ahead on the ridge: pass a path down to the right (signposted Minso) but follow the main ridge passing Bocca Culaghia and Punta Culaghia. After some time this ridge is left by means of a very steep couloir to descend to a wide valley. It is also possible to reach Haut Asco from the foot of this couloir by continuing down the valley for 25 minutes. The GR20 bears off up the valley and continues to an area of loose rocks in the vicinity of Altore beneath the imposing Col Perdu.

Spasimata Valley Photo: D.Unsworth

Taking the plunge in the waters of Le Golo. Deep pools in the mountain streams offer cold refreshment, contrasting sharply with the midday heat of the barren surroundings. Photo: D.Unsworth

DAY 3

ALTORE to MORI

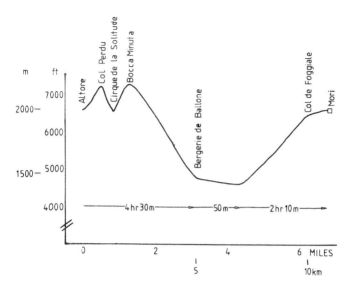

DAY 3: ALTORE TO MORI

DISTANCE:	6.7 miles (10.8km)
ASCENT:	3,396ft (1,034m)
DESCENT:	3,396ft (1,034m)
TIME:	7hrs 30mins
GRADE:	Cirque de la Solitude is Grade D. The remainder of the route is mainly Grade B.

This section contains a traverse of the famous Cirque de la Solitude, under the impressive west face of Minuta. This is certainly the crux of the walk, and to make the crossing unaided would require one to climb at Alpine Grade 1+ (roughly equivalent to the rock climbing grade of Moderate on the British system). However, the route has

been protected by a series of fixed ropes, cables and chains, making it possible for the average walker, with a head for heights, to do the traverse without too many problems. The entire crossing is over steep and barren rocks, slabs and boulders and unless you are an experienced rock climber it is absolutely essential to follow the marked route. Whilst descending into the Cirque it may seem that there is no easy way out, but careful following of the red and white markers will lead you safely to Bocca Minuta. The Cirque de la Solitude is one of the few places in Europe where the walker can experience the exposure of steep granite crags and delve right in amongst towering cliffs and rocky spires, an environment usually preserved for the mountain climber.

Great care must be exercised whilst in the Cirque de la Solitude as rocks and stones can easily be dislodged with disastrous consequences for anyone below. Remember your position; you are a long way from civilisation and help. Despite its name, the Cirque is usually a very crowded place with queues forming at the chains in the main season. Do not rush this section; it is a beautiful, albeit austere place and its crossing will almost certainly be a lifelong memory.

The descent from Bocca Minuta down the Viro Valley is long and the knees will probably take a pounding. The scenery makes up for this and is of the first class. The river which is met lower down is a good place for a cooling dip, followed by a sunbathe on the surrounding rocks. The Bergerie de Ballone is occupied for much of the main season and is one of the few places on route where food (mainly cheese and ham sandwiches and fruit drinks) may be purchased. It is also usually permitted to camp or bivouac in this area, where there is ample water supply. Note that a new refuge has now been built in this area (this is not shown on maps prior to 1986). There follows an easy walk mainly through woodland (again much damaged by fires) before turning westwards for a hard climb up to the Col de Foggiale. You will want to rest many times on this ascent to admire the superb vistas behind you across the valley. On reaching the Col there are impressive views over the next valley and it is now a relatively easy stroll across to the Mori hut beneath the

Looking from the Col Perdu to the Cirque de la Solitude. The Paglia Orba is the dominating peak; the smaller one being Capu Tafunatu. Photo: D.Unsworth

Capu Tafunatu and Paglia Orba from the Golo Valley.
Photo: D.Unsworth

crags of the mighty Tafunatu, a popular mountain for rock climbers. The hut, which carries solar panels, is close to the course of the River Golo, one of the main rivers on the north of the island. Note that the water source at the Mori Refuge sometimes dries up at the end of a very hot summer. It is then necessary to make the long descent to the River Golo for water.

The Mori Refuge could be used as a base from which to climb Paglia Orba (8,292ft-2,525m) via the waymarked route to the Col des Maures. This ascent requires a considerable amount of scrambling of a high technical standard and should only be tackled by experienced parties.

Route

Follow the red and white markers to the left of the burnt-out Altore hut and within 5 minutes pass a water source. Continue upwards passing the two small mountain lakes of Col Perdu. Pick a way over the loose rocks and stones to the summit of Col Perdu. Descend very steeply down into the Cirque de la Solitude, *following the red and*

Cirque de la Solitude, northern side. Photo: D.Unsworth

white markers, and making full use of the fixed ropes and chains. After a drop of about 700ft, the route begins to climb the wall of the Cirque. The difficulty is maintained and you will find the fixed cables most useful. Nearing the top (about 800ft of climbing) the gradient eases slightly up to Bocca Minuta. From here continue southwards down a rocky path towards the Viro Valley. Just after arriving at the first pines, you will come to the Bergerie de Ballone. There are several confusing paths in this area, so be sure to follow the red and white signs carefully from the Bergerie. Continue on a good forested path and slowly swing towards the west. Here begins an arduous climb up to the summit of the Col de Foggiale. Follow the red and white markings on the rocks to the top of the Col where bear slightly to the right (do not descend at this point). The route climbs gently until in a short while, on reaching a slight rise, the Mori hut becomes visible. This is then reached within 10 minutes.

Approach to the Manganu Refuge

DAY 4

MORI to MANGANU

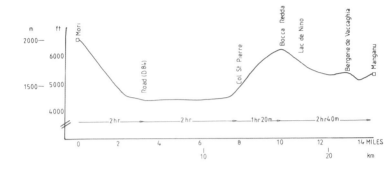

DAY 4: MORI TO MANGANU

DISTANCE:	14.5 miles (23.4km)
ASCENT:	2,095ft (638m)
DESCENT:	3,402ft (1,036m)
TIME:	8hrs
GRADE:	Mainly Grade A with some Grade B.

Today's journey is a long one and it may be that after the rigours of the last few days you wish to break this into two very easy days. This is possible by making a slight detour when coming out at a road near the Col de Vergio, to reach the Hôtel Castel di Vergio. This is signposted and is about 1.25 miles off the GR20. The hotel will provide all the luxuries of civilisation including a bath, non-dehydrated food and a bed for the night. If you feel that you can do without such pampering and you are still feeling fit, then you should find that the whole route to the Manganu hut is not too arduous. There is only one major climb of about 2,000ft in all, and

DAY 4: MORI TO MANGANU

by Corsican standards this is not particularly steep. Much of the route is more or less on the level and so you should be able to enjoy the splendid scenery without too much exertion. Make the most of this gentle area; there is more serious climbing to follow!

The route leaves the Mori hut and descends to a spectacular valley, crossing the River Golo several times to emerge eventually at a road. This is the first road since Bonifato, three days ago. The GR20 continues on a more or less level woodland path for several miles with superb mountain views over on the left-hand side. Eventually the route ascends to the shrine at Col St. Petru where there are distant views of mountain peaks and a wide, forested valley. After a further climb to Bocca Redda, the path descends to the picturesque Lac de Nino. Here is a wide grassy area, which provides an excellent spot for a picnic (note that camping is strictly forbidden in this area). An hour can be lazed away watching cattle and horses grazing whilst admiring the distant views of rocky mountain ranges. From here easy walking takes one past an old demolished cabin, then a bergerie and on to the Manganu hut. This is situated by a bridge over the river and provides stunning views of central high Corsica.

Route

Leave the Mori hut by one of two paths. The one that descends straight from the hut is quicker but the one that leaves the hut on the level and later descends is the more scenic and is to be recommended in fine weather. These two paths soon meet up to follow gently down the valley with a stream on the left. Later the red and white waymarks take one across this river to continue down a stony path with the stream on the right. Somewhat later the stream is re-crossed and the waymarks are followed until the path, now through woodland, emerges at a road (the D84) at a hairpin bend. For the Hôtel Castel di Vergio turn right here and follow the road for 1.25 miles (2km) with only 246ft (75m) of ascent.

To continue on the GR20 turn right on the road at the hairpin bend for a few yards and pick up a path running between roads. Follow this path through pine woodland. Be very careful not to lose the red and white waymarks as there are several paths through these woods. Continue on this woodland path maintaining a height

The unusually wide Tavignano Valley with Lac Nino, seen from the summit of Capu a u Tozzu. In the distance is the Monte Rotondo massif. Photo: D.Unsworth

of approximately 4,500ft (1,370m) above sea level. After 5 miles (8.1km) leave this level path on the right and head uphill through trees to reach the Col St Petru (Col St Pierre) where there is a shrine to the saint. This is really a shoulder of a higher ridge and the GR20 takes this to climb beneath an electricity pylon. A good zigzagging path continues upwards through more woodland to arrive eventually at the summit of Bocca Redda. The path traverses the top and carries on down to the delightful Lac de Nino.

Pass the lake on an easy path which gradually goes downhill to reach some trees and the Ancient Refuge de Campiglione. Here there are only the remains of one wall and a disused water trough. Follow the waymarks to the Bergerie de Vaccaghia which is a stone building with a good source of water. Your destination for the night (the Refuge de Manganu) is visible from here across the Plan de Compotile. The hut is reached by crossing this area, descending at first and then walking uphill to a bridge across the stream just before the hut.

*Monte d'Oro seen in evening light from the Refuge de Pietra-Piana.
Photo: D.Unsworth*

DAY 5

MANGANU to PIETRA-PIANA

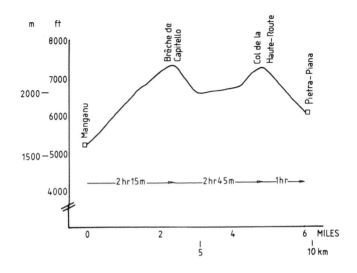

DAY 5: MANGANU TO PIETRA-PIANA

DISTANCE:	6.0 miles (9.7km)
ASCENT:	2,762ft (841m)
DESCENT:	1,967ft (599m)
TIME:	6hrs
GRADE:	A mixture of Grade B & C. The ridge route from Brêche de Capitello to the Col de la Haute-Route requires particular care.

This is a superb section of the GR20 amid fluted rocky spires and ridges. After a steep climb over rocks and boulders up to the Brêche de Capitello the route follows a rocky ridge with tremendous views of several other granite ridges, and two mountain lakes below. This section should not be rushed for two reasons. Firstly a slip here could have very serious consequences and all care should be exercised. Secondly the scenery is of the highest order and so allow

The view from Col de la Haute-Route with Col de Rinoso and Lac de Rinoso in the foreground. Beyond can be seen the massive rock buttress of Capitello and pinnacled northern ridge of Punte alle Porte which the route crosses. Photo: D.Unsworth

plenty of time for stopping and staring. The route follows a classic horseshoe ridge and on approaching the Col de Rinoso, a third small lake comes into view. A little further on brings one to the Col de la Haute Route, the highest point on the GR20. From here there is a steep rocky descent down the mountainside until eventually the Pietra-Piana hut is reached. This is a relatively small hut with space for about twenty people, but with a very small dining room. However, there is a fairly large, flat, enclosed area which is suitable for camping (the fencing makes it pig-free, an important consideration). The hut acts as one of the bases for the mountain rescue service and has its own helicopter landing area.

It would be possible for a very fit party to combine today's route with tomorrow's itinerary to L'Onda. This would nevertheless make for a long day and since the scenery is of such a high order, most parties will prefer to settle for two relatively short days.

Another possibility is to use the Pietra-Piana hut as a base whilst making an ascent of Monte Rotondo (8,611ft-2,622m). There is a

Lac de Melo and surrounding ridge

rough, cairned route which requires some scrambling ability.

Route
Leave the hut and re-cross the bridge. Follow the waymarked path upwards to a high grassy plateau which is reached in about 30 minutes. Continue over boulders and along a stony path to head eventually for a cleft in the rocky ridge above. From here (the Brêche de Capitello) there are fine views of granite ridges and the route ahead; to the left and below will be seen the Lac de Capitello and the Lac de Melo. Descend with care; this is quite a tricky scramble in places and there are no fixed supports. Follow the red and white waymarks to skirt above the two lakes with more rocky spires and ridges coming into view. Continue along this mountain path which later becomes somewhat easier. The route unfolds as a 'horseshoe' until eventually it climbs to the Col de Rinoso. From here continue on to the Col de la Haute-Route at 7,245ft (2,206m). Carry on over

Crossing the Manganello river by a log bridge en route for Monte Rotondo. Photo: D.Unsworth

Bergerie de Tolla towards Monte Rotondo. Photo: D.Unsworth

this col and descend steeply maintaining a south-easterly direction until the Pietra-Piana hut comes into view below. Approach this via the gates through the enclosure, just before the hut.

Pietra-Piana   Photo: D.Unsworth

DAY 6

PIETRA-PIANA
to
L'ONDA

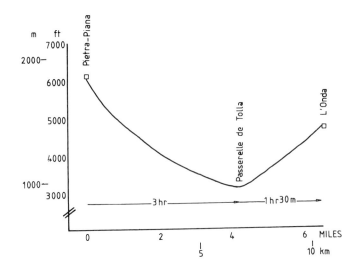

DAY 6: PIETRA-PIANA TO L'ONDA

DISTANCE:	6.5 miles (10.4km)
ASCENT:	1,642ft (500m)
DESCENT:	2,995ft (912m)
TIME:	4hrs 30mins
GRADE:	B

This is a short and relatively easy day (really only a half-day) and will provide plenty of time for lying around in the sun admiring the views. For those who have had enough of the sun, there is quite a long section through picturesque pine and deciduous forest providing considerable shade. This section is in admirable contrast to the rocky scrambling of yesterday.

The route consists of a very long descent from the hut, most of which is of a gentle gradient. Just before the river at the low point

Refuge De Manganu
Lac de Capitello and Lac de Melo

Monte Rotondo makes a rewarding excursion from the GR20.
View south from just below the summit.
Brêche de Capitello

Refuge L'Ortu Di u Piobbu
Monte Cinto and the rugged Corsican peaks from near Capu Ladroncellu.

In the Cirque de la Solitude below Bocca Minuta.
The path south of Bocca Minuta.

The Bergerie de Vaccaghia (Day 4). Like others along the route, this provides camping space and sells cheese to hungry wayfarers.
Photo: D.Unsworth

of our walk a bergerie is reached which may sell simple food (eg. snacks of bread and cheese) but don't rely on it. After this there is a moderate climb first on a forest track and later coming out onto open hillside, until the hut of L'Onda comes into view ahead. There is a bergerie close to the hut and if the latter is full, additional accommodation may be available at the bergerie. There is also an excellent enclosed camping area here.

There is an alternative route which is shorter but which stays to high ground and follows the mountain ridges. This variation leaves the main route just below the Pietra-Piana hut and rejoins it at L'Onda. This route would save time (about 45 minutes) but it lacks the contrast of scenery provided by the main route, and is not to be recommended in bad weather.

Route
From the Pietra-Piana hut go back across the enclosure and follow

the waymarks down into the valley. The route is quite steep at first descending to the bergerie buildings (notice the branch point for the alternative path going off to the right). Continue on a stony path crossing three streams and with impressive granite crags on the left-hand wall of the valley. Eventually the tree-line is reached and there follows a gentle walk through woodland for several miles. At the 3,284ft (1,000m) mark the Bergerie de Tolla is reached and 0.25 of a mile further down cross the river by means of a suspension bridge. Begin the ascent on a wide forest track with the sound of the fast-flowing river over to the right. This later becomes a path and one continues upwards through the trees. Eventually as one comes out of the trees the hut is seen at a higher level away in the distance. After passing through further small belts of trees the Bergerie de L'Onda is reached and just above this is the hut of the same name.

Monte d'Oro from Bocca Palmente. Photo: D.Unsworth

DAY 7

L'ONDA
to
VIZZAVONA

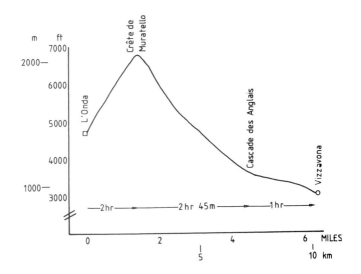

DAY 7: L'ONDA TO VIZZAVONA

DISTANCE:	6.3 miles (10.1km)
ASCENT:	2,082ft (634m)
DESCENT:	3,757ft (1,144m)
TIME:	5hrs 45mins
GRADE:	B

It is recommended that an early start is made from L'Onda so that Vizzavona is reached by lunchtime. This will provide a half-day break to relax, unwind, buy provisions, and generally 're-charge the batteries'. There is a choice of simple hotels to stay at and you can spoil yourself by having a bath or shower with hot water that comes from the tap! Yes, you are in civilisation again. It is also an excellent

The path lies close to the Cascade des Anglais through delightful pine woods. In the background is Monte d'Oro. Photo: D.Unsworth

opportunity to sample Corsican cooking, so why not treat yourself to a slap-up lunch and dinner. You will probably be ravenously hungry, and it is a good idea to get some roughage inside you after all that dehydrated food!.

But before you can sample the heady delights of Vizzavona you have a hard walk in front of you. From the hut there is a steep, relentless climb up to the Crête de Muratello. From here there are once again superb views of the surrounding mountains and over to Corse de Sud, the southern section of the island, which is your next objective. From the Crête you look down into the wooded valley of Vizzavona way below and it is here that you must go, threading slowly down over slabs, rocks and boulders to reach a bridge over the river at the Cascade des Anglais. Do not underestimate this descent; it may look a stone's throw away from the Crête to the valley, but it generally takes a long, long time to get down. Be sure to look behind you many times during the descent to admire the granite peaks you have now left behind. From the bridge it is an easy stroll down into the village.

From just after the Crête de Muratello it is possible to follow a route to the summit of Monte D'Oro (7,846ft-2,389m). This route is waymarked in places but requires a considerable amount of scrambling, some quite difficult in nature. It would make a fine excursion for a sufficiently experienced party in good weather.

Vizzavona is roughly the halfway mark of the GR20, although in fact you have walked a little more than half of the total route and most of what follows is generally of an easier standard than the trail in the north. Vizzavona conveniently splits the Haute-Corse section from the Corse de Sud. Without this small village with its road and rail connections and the possibility to buy provisions, the GR20 would be a far more severe challenge.

Route

Leave L'Onda hut and ascend across the mountainside to a sign on a large rock pointing to Vizzavona. Ascend on a steep path with a deep wooded valley over to the right and impressive rocky ridges ahead. The path is steep but good. After about 1 hour 30 minutes of ascent the path zigzags up to the Crête de Muratello which should be reached after about 2 hours of effort. The descent is steep over

DAY 7: L'ONDA TO VIZZAVONA

rocks and large granite slabs at first and later it becomes a path descending over rocks and boulders and passing several small waterfalls. Eventually the river is crossed by a wooden bridge and the way continues with this boulder stream now on the left. The path remains rough for much of the way (slabs, boulders and rocks) but lower down there are several good picnic sites on the large boulders by the river, as you descend through the trees. Eventually you will reach a large bridge at the Cascade des Anglais to re-cross the river. The path is now smooth and gently descends through the trees. This later becomes a track which is followed through several bends, with a few gentle ascents and descents until the road is reached at a bend. It is here (Maison de la Forestière) where you pay for the nearby camping site and there is also a forest information office in the same building. Turn left on the road and after a few yards turn left off the road on a footpath signposted *gare*. Follow this down through woodland to arrive at a road by a delightful chapel (built in 1931). Turn left here to enter the village of Vizzavona.

Pines and mountains above Vizzavona

DAY 8

VIZZAVONA to CAPANELLE

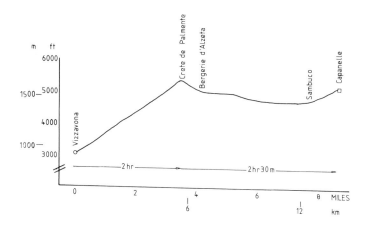

DAY 8: VIZZAVONA TO CAPANELLE

DISTANCE: 8.6 miles (13.7km)
ASCENT: 2,782ft (847m)
DESCENT: 614ft (187m)
TIME: 4hrs 30mins
GRADE: Vizzavona to Col de Palmente is Grade B. The remainder is Grade A.

This is a most pleasant stage with no real difficulties. The route begins with a long climb through the Vizzavona forest, but on good tracks and paths and with superb views over the Vizzavona Valley to Monte D'Oro and its surrounding peaks. On reaching the Col de Palmente at 5,376ft (1,637m) there is a fine contrast between the high granite peaks of Haute Corse that you have now left behind, with the more gentle wooded hills of Corse de Sud. The GR20 takes a pleasant path from here through pine woods with many chances to admire the fine mountain scenery. The last section to the Capanelle hut involves a steep but short climb through woodland. Nearby the hut there is a ski-lift and a bar/restaurant which also sells backpackers' provisions.

The Capanelle hut would form an excellent base to climb the nearby Monte Renoso (7,731ft-2,354m). This is a relatively easy walking ascent and takes about 2 hours 15 minutes to reach the summit from the hut. A recommended scrambling traverse of the mountain can be made to return by a different route to the Capanelle hut in a further 2 hours 15 minutes. Details of this excursion are given in the Collomb guide to Corsica (see Bibliography).

Route

Retrace your steps in Vizzavona past the chapel and up the woodland path to the road. Turn left and walk downhill on the road for about 300 yards (274 metres) and turn right on to a forest track signposted 'GR20 Sud'. Continue on this gentle track following the GR20 signs and the red and white markers for about 20 minutes when you leave the track to go up on a zigzag path. After about 30 minutes through this pine and deciduous woodland the path comes out at a track on a bend. Cross over this track and continue to zigzag upwards through woodland. Eventually the path comes out of the trees and skirts the hillside to reach the Col de Palmente in about 2 hours from Vizzavona.

A good path continues around the hillside to the Bergerie D'Alzeta (cheese and wine may be for sale here, but do not rely on it). Continue, still on a good path, passing through trees and over the Crête de Cardo. The route takes the form of a large horseshoe. After a while the path drops a little, crosses a stream and passes the Bergerie de Scarpaccedie. After another 10 minutes or so you start to climb steeply through woodland. Emerging from this to reach a road, turn right for 200 yards (183 metres) and look for a sign indicating 'GR Sud' on the left. Follow the signs down to the Refuge Capanelle.

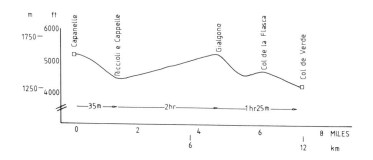

DAY 9

CAPANELLE
to
COL DE VERDE

DAY 9: CAPANELLE TO COL DE VERDE

DISTANCE:	7.3 miles (11.8km)
ASCENT:	923ft (281m)
DESCENT:	1,911ft (582m)
TIME:	4hrs
GRADE:	A

Today's journey is a short and easy one with very little climbing and all on good paths. It would be perfectly possible for a fit party to combine yesterday's route with this one to give a fairly long but relatively easy stage from the road at Vizzavona to that at the Col de Verde.

Another alternative would be to combine today's journey with the first part of tomorrow's itinerary to the Refuge de Prati, although this would require a fairly strenuous climb up to the Col de Prati in the heat of the afternoon. Furthermore, it would mean that you missed out on the fine evening's hospitality provided at the bar/restaurant on the Col de Verde. It would, however, leave you with a fairly short day to follow, in order to savour the superb ridge walk from Prati to D'Usciolu.

Route

Leave the refuge and follow the path to descend to the river passing first the Bergerie de Traggette over on the right (this is quite a large complex). On reaching the road turn right over the bridge, and in a few yards pick up a path on the right. Continue gently up with extensive views of the mountains over to the left and back over much of the route that you completed yesterday. This pleasant path provides plenty of tree shade and following it will eventually lead to the plateau of Gialgone. Here there is a descent down the Marmano Valley by a zigzag path which could be wet in places near the small tributaries. At the river go over by a boulder crossing. Just past this point you will pass some very large, old pine trees that have enormously thick trunks. There follows a gentle climb to the Col de la Flascia and finally a gentle descent through a forest which is cleared in places. Come out at a road where there is a privately owned refuge and a nearby bar/restaurant.

Ridge in the region of Punta Capella

DAY 10

COL DE VERDE to D'USCIOLU

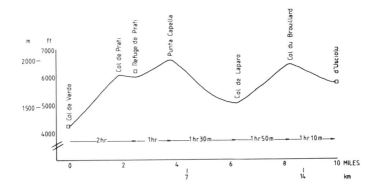

DAY 10: COL DE VERDE TO D'USCIOLU

DISTANCE:	9.9 miles (15.9km)
ASCENT:	3,796ft (1,156m)
DESCENT:	2,282ft (695m)
TIME:	7hrs 30mins
GRADE:	B (some short stretches of C on the ridge)

After a fairly steep climb up through the Vizzavona forest to the Col de Prati there follows a pleasant walk on a high level, granite-strewn plateau. The Prati hut is situated here and is a good place to fill your water bottles, as there is not another water source on the route until the Refuge D'Usciolu. From the Prati the granite ridge ahead is climbed and followed all the way to your destination for the day. This is a walk of the highest order with distant views of the coast out to the left and a wide, inhabited, wooded valley down to the right, stretching back to the Col de Verde. Most of the ridge is easily traversed but there are one or two places where hands may be necessary. The region is not unlike the tops of the Glyders in North Wales, but on a much grander scale and with prickly maquis below, rather than grass and bilberry. The hut D'Usciolu is in a fine

Mountains and trees from near the Col de Laparo

situation amidst the mountains and it is advisable to arrive not too late in the afternoon in order to spend a lazy hour or two basking in the sunshine on the veranda.

Route
Cross the road and go up the wide forest track opposite. After 10 minutes leave this track for a woodland path on the left. Climb on this well-defined path through the wood, until you arrive out of the trees on a pleasant plateau with fine views of mountains behind. The route maintains height to the left of a small valley, before zigzagging steeply to the Col de Prati. Here bear right for a pleasant walk on the plateau to reach the Prati hut. Take special note that this is the last water source until D'Usciolu (there is no water on the ridge).

From the hut follow the sign to D'Usciolu and cross the plateau towards the peaks. Climb onto the ridge (steeply at the end) and then proceed along the arête, picking your way carefully over rocks, boulders and slabs to Punta Capella. Eventually descend onto an open col (Col de Rapari) passing a small metal cross on the right dedicated to a walker killed at this spot in 1983. At the Col ensure that you take the correct path (there are others). Descend passing through two small areas of woodland to come to another sign indicating the Refuge D'Usciolu (in 3 hours 15 minutes) and the Refuge Prati (2 hours 30 minutes back in the direction you have just travelled). Here there is also a signposted path down to the left to San Gavino in 2 hours 30 minutes. Just 10 minutes down this path will bring you to a new refuge, with a water source a few minutes walk below. Finally a path leads off the ridge down to the right to San Antoine (in 1 hour 45 minutes). Continuing on the path to D'Usciolu you will soon begin to climb fairly steeply. There is a fair bit of shade given at first by a number of trees along the way. Come out of the trees and continue the ascent to the top of the ridge. Follow the path along the ridge with views left, out to the lower, eastern hills and the sea. Eventually make a short descent to the hut D'Usciolu.

Looking west from just below Bocca Minuta, Cirque de la Solitude

Bergerie di Ballone
Capu Tafunatu and Paglia Orba from the south.

The bridge below the Bergerie de Tolla.

Bellebone Lake from below the summit of Monte Rotondo.

*Crête de Muratello from the top of the Vizzavona Valley.
Looking north along the Monte Incudine ridge*

Refuge d'Usciolu

DAY 11

D'USCIOLU
to
D'ASINAO

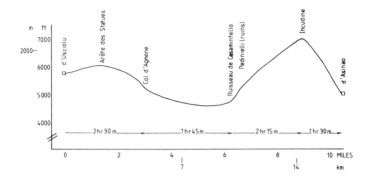

DAY 11: D'USCIOLU TO D'ASINAO

DISTANCE:	10.4 miles (16.8km)
ASCENT:	2,581ft (786m)
DESCENT:	3,304ft (1,006m)
TIME:	8hrs
GRADE:	Mainly B with short sections of Grade C on the ridge at the start of the trail. The path from the Col D'Agnone to the River Casamintello is Grade A. The descent from Incudine is very steep and if the waymarked route is lost then difficulties are greatly increased.

The first section of today's route resumes the ridge to provide easy scrambling with superb views. A descent from this ridge through woodland leads to a pleasant plateau which is gently descended to another suspension bridge over the River Casamintello. Here is an excellent spot for a bathe in the cool river, followed by a picnic lunch. There then begins an ascent of Incudine via the demolished hut of Pedinelli. Incudine is the only true mountain summit on the whole of the classic route of the GR20. From the cross on the barren top of the mountain there is a magnificent panorama of the Corsican mountains. Definitely a spot to linger. But don't stay there too long because there follows a very steep, tedious descent to the Refuge D'Asinao. This hut will be seen soon after you leave the summit ridge, but it will take a long time before you are stretched out on the veranda soaking in the sun, gazing at the fluted granite ridges all around. Note the pine trees growing on the top of the distant ridge to the left: these at first glance look like thin rock pinnacles from a distance. Stay out on this veranda and watch the sun set below the mountains and stare at the night sky with its multitude of stars. You should also make out far down in the valley the lights of the village of Quenza. This is the sign that your time in the wilderness is soon to be over, as we are now no more than two days from the end of your journey across the mountains of Corsica.

Route

Leave D'Usciolu hut and ascend to the granite ridge on the right. Follow the ridge south-westwards. After about 20 minutes you will reach a sign to Cozzaro down to the right (in 2 hours 30 minutes). This descending trail is marked with yellow flashes. For the GR20 continue on the ridge with distant views out to sea on the left and the large wooded valley on the right, stretching back to the trees of the Col de Verde. After about 1 hours 20 minutes there is a steep but short ascent to a wooden cross on a granite summit, where there is also a low stone IGN mark (pretty insignificant compared with our own OS triangulation stones). Continue along the ridge and after about 15 minutes ascend a short, steep gully to cross over on to the right-hand side of the ridge. Make a final descent from this ridge to enter some trees, where at the col there is a sign back to D'Usciolu (in 2 hours 45 minutes) and on to the Refuge Pedinelli (2 hours 15 minutes). A pleasant path leads through these trees to come out at an open plateau with views ahead of the next stage of the walk. Continue along this undulating plateau, crossing several streams. Just before one of these is a sign indicating a diversion to a nearby bergerie, where cheese and snacks may be purchased. The route to this bergerie is marked with prominent red flashes. If this is ignored then continue on the GR20 to cross a track. The path meets a second track where you bear right for about 30 metres before turning off left to follow the path to a suspension bridge over the river (Ruisseau de Casamintello). If you followed the variation to the bergerie then there is a direct path from there to the suspension bridge (again marked with red flashes).

From the suspension bridge begin climbing first through woodland and then up to the Refuge Pedinelli (this was completely destroyed some years ago and only the foundations now remain). Note that the water at the Pedinelli hut is polluted, but that there is a source 5 minutes higher on the GR trail. Proceeed on a good mountain path to the Col de Luana. Here an impressive rocky combe opens out with a stream running down the middle. The mountain that heads the combe is the Punta di Tintennaja (6,627ft-2,018m) but the GR20 keeps to the right-hand side and heads for Incudine further away. Continue up the ridge. The waymarks are a little indistinct here and several narrow paths abound, but generally going up the ridge should eventually bring you to the summit of Incudine (7,008ft-2,134m). This is a giant granite mound topped by a stone cross. Traverse the summit ridge and descend for about 20 minutes until a sign is reached pointing to the left and down to the Refuge D'Asinao. The sign indicates a time of 1 hour 30 minutes to the hut from here, but as you can see the refuge from this point you may disbelieve the sign. However, the steep descent is very tedious and requires care. Follow the red and white waymarks carefully down the mountainside. Take special care not to lose these signs as they are fairly indistinct near the top. Descend over slabs, boulders and rocks. Eventually a more distinct path is reached and this leads down to the hut.

Notre Dame de la Neige, Col de Bavella

DAY 12

D'ASINAO to PALIRI

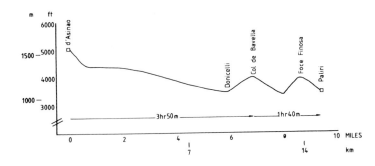

DAY 12: D'ASINAO TO PALIRI

DISTANCE:	9.3 miles (15.0km)
ASCENT:	1,146ft (394m)
DESCENT:	2,591ft (789m)
TIME:	5hrs 30mins
GRADE:	B (the variation is C/D)

The highlight of today's itinerary is the magnificent rock scenery of the Col de Bavella. This gem of the southern half of Corsica is situated on a road and unfortunately can become very crowded in summer with coach loads of tourists. The Col divides a superb range of rock needles into two parts, and all around the scenery is first rate with many fine red towers and pinnacles. The picturesque Col makes a fine place for a picnic. Immediately below the pass is a small settlement of wooden huts and cabins called the Village de Bavella. These are the summer residences of the inhabitants of Conca who were granted occupational rights by Napoleon III. Here too can be found a couple of café/restaurants and an épicerie where a plentiful supply of groceries can be bought.

To get to the Col de Bavella involves a descent from Asinao followed by a series of woodland paths to skirt the high rocky Pargolu Spur, with fine views down to the wooded side valleys, and of the towering rock pinnacles above. A low point is reached at the Donicelli stream and then there is a steady climb up to the Bavella pass.

At the Col de Bavella

There is a variation to the standard route which involves some moderate scrambling (with a chain for assistance over the most difficult section) and a further climb of 1,133ft (345m). This alternative, which is somewhat shorter than the standard route, is to be recommended in fine weather providing breathtaking views of the rocky towers and spires of the Pargolu shoulder and of Bavella. This variation leaves the main route at about the 4,300ft (1,309m) mark and is clearly waymarked with double yellow flashes.

South of the Col de Bavella the scenery is still first rate with numerous granite towers and pinnacles to delight the eyes, particularly the splendid Paliri towers in the vicinity of the Paliri Refuge, the most southerly hut in Corsica.

Route
Descend from the D'Asinao hut on a rock-strewn path, after 15 minutes passing a sign indicating the village of Quenza (4 hours). This path goes off to the right and is signposted with yellow flashes. The GR20 bears to the left and soon crosses a river. Continue on an undulating path through the trees on the left-hand side of the valley.

Rocky slabs on the approach to the Refuge de Paliri

After about 1 hours 10 minutes from the hut the point is reached where the alternative route leaves the standard way. The variation is off to the left and is signposted 'Variante Alpisme, Col de Bavella 4 hours'. The standard route, marked with the usual red and white stripes continues on a good path again undulating, but gently heading down the left-hand side of the Asinao Valley through the maquis, with views over to the right of the wooded foothills. The path soon begins to turn and the rocky spires of the Cornes D'Asinao come into view. The path rises and falls gradually, giving impressive views of the rocky Crête de Pargolu until there is a final climb up to the road at the Col de Bavella, where you emerge at a stone cross and a nearby Madonna (Notre Dame de la Neige).

Follow the paths down through the wooded huts of the Village de Bavella to rejoin the road where there are two cafés and a grocer's shop. Take the old track that leads off the bend in the road (signposted Refuge Paliri 2 hours 30 minutes). After about 10 minutes take a marked path down to the left. Follow this until it meets a crossing track where turn right. Continue over a concrete bridge round a hairpin bend. Soon take a path that leads upwards, zigzagging to

DAY 12: D'ASINAO TO PALIRI

the Foce Finosa where there is a superb view down the valley. Follow the zigzag path downwards until you reach the Paliri hut at 3,415ft (1,040m) on a small cleared plateau. The water source is some 200 yards before the hut (in dry weather this can be reduced to a mere trickle).

Rock pinnacles in the Paliri region

DAY 13

PALIRI
to
CONCA

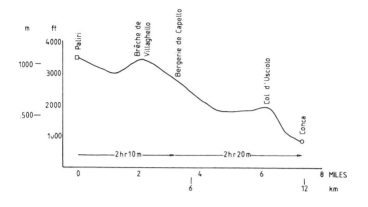

DAY 13: PALIRI TO CONCA

DISTANCE: 7.3 miles (11.8km)
ASCENT: 565ft (172m)
DESCENT: 3,284ft (1,000m)
TIME: 4hrs 30mins
GRADE: B

The last section of the GR20 to its termination at the small hill town of Conca is mainly a long descent out of the southern Corsican mountains and should present no major problems. The waymarking can be a little difficult to follow in places, so some concentration on route-finding is required. There is one fairly steep ascent which could come as a surprise for anyone under the assumption that it is downhill all the way. But this climb is quite short and the descent is once more resumed.

The scenery during the first part of the descent is of a very high quality with rock towers and granite ridges abounding, but unfortunately the last 2 or 3 miles to the very outskirts of Conca suffered a devastating fire in the summer of 1985. When the route

View of the mountains of Southern Corsica from the Paliri region

was walked by the author in September 1985 the whole area was severely burned and a smell of burnt timber and maquis hung heavily on the air. It will take many years for the complete natural regeneration of the area.

Conca is a small pleasant town lying at the foot of the mountains of southern Corsica, some 15 miles (24.2km) from the town of Porto-Vecchio on the coast. Conca does not have any hotels, nor does it have a bus service. There is a campsite and a bar/restaurant (Le Soleil Levant) within 100 yards of the church in the centre of the town. This café has a public telephone which would enable you to phone for a taxi. Alternatively an easy road walk of about 3.5 miles (5.8km) takes you to Sainte-Lucie de Porto-Vecchio, which is on the main road from Porto-Vecchio to Bastia (RN 198). From here a bus may be taken either to Porto-Vecchio or to Bastia (usually two buses a day in both directions).

Route
Near the Paliri hut there is a sign indicating the direction to Conca.

Rocky spires and slabs near the Col de Monte Bracciuto

Pass through pine woodland on a good smooth path. Pass several granite outcrops and pause in several places to admire the splendid views of granite ridges and towers over to the left. Continue down through more woodland providing plenty of shade from the sun. After some time there is a short, steep climb of about 400 feet (122m) to reach the Brêche de Villaghello, the last climb of any note on the GR20. Care is needed on the granite plateau after this brêche, as it is easy to lose the route. Follow a series of cairns and old, worn red and white stripes. Continue through maquis and sparse trees, passing several granite outcrops (some with quite weird shapes) to the ruins of the Bergerie de Capello (2,791ft-850m).

After this the route crosses areas of maquis and pine to pass two river tributaries. The first tributary marks the beginning of the 1985 fire damage. From the second tributary (last water before the fountain at Conca) take the zigzag path which climbs somewhat to cross the ridge to begin a long, sweeping path which undulates gently and clings to the upper right-hand side of the valley. This area was very badly burned in August, 1985. The path describes a wide arc to arrive at the Col D'Usciolo through a narrow cleft in a large rock. From this point the village of Conca is clearly visible in the densely-wooded valley below. Descend through woodland to emerge at a road just after a water fountain. Turn left here and descend through the outskirts of Conca to arrive at the church after about a mile (1.6km) of road walking.

APPENDIX 1 MOUNTAIN HUTS ON THE GR20

All of the huts have a water source close-by, but note that some of these can sometimes dry up in very hot weather.

The huts have a 'unisex' sleeping area (dormitory bunks) and a sitting room/kitchen. Calor gas stoves are standard and each hut has an assortment of crockery and cutlery. Illumination is normally by candlelight or from calor gas lamps. Many huts are equipped with solar panels. There are toilet facilities at each hut and litter can usually be left for disposal. Camping is often allowed in the vicinity of the hut for a nominal fee. The overnight charge is the same for all the huts. All are run by the PNR (except where indicated) and have resident wardens during the main season.

Refuge L'Ortu Di u Piobbu

Situated east-south-east of the Capu Ghiovu to the south-east of Calenzana. A new hut (opened in the late 1980s) on the new section of the GR20 between Calenzana and Spasimata.

Refuge Spasimata

Situated south-east of the Bonifato roadhead beneath the Punta di Spasimata. Altitude 3,904ft (1,190m). 10.1 miles (16.2km) from Calenzana; 99.2 miles (159.7km) from Conca. 8.9 miles (14.3km) 10.5 hours to the next hut (Ballone). Approximately twenty-five sleeping places. Hut opened in 1984. There is a cold shower outside the hut.

Refuge De L'Altore

This important, strategically placed hut (in a rocky cwm beneath and to the north of Col Perdu) was destroyed by fire in 1985. Camping on hard ground is possible in the vicinity. There is a good water supply in the area.

'Refuge de Ballone'

Situated below and to the south of the Cirque de la Solitude. Altitude approx. 5,000ft (1,525m). 19 miles (30.6km) from Calenzana; 90.3 miles (145.3km) from Conca. 8.9 miles (14.3km) from the last hut (Spasimata); 4.2 miles (6.8km) to the next hut (Mori). This new refuge was built in the late 1980s to replace that of Altore destroyed in 1985.

Refuge Ciottulu Di i Mori
Situated below the Col des Maures and between the peaks of Tafonato and Paglia Orba. Altitude 6,562ft (2,000m). 23.2 miles (37.4km) from Calenzana; 86.1 miles (138.6km) from Conca. 4.2 miles (6.8km). 3.0 hours from last hut (Ballone); 14.5 miles (23.3km) 8 hours to next hut (Manganu). Approximately twenty-four sleeping places. The hut is equipped with solar panels. The water source can run dry in very hot weather. The next available source is the River Golo, a 45-minute round trip from the hut. Mori is often frequented by climbing parties.

Refuge De Manganu
Situated on the south-east of Bocca d'Acqua Ciarnente. Altitude 5,249ft (1,600m) 37.7 miles (60.7km) from Calenzana; 71.6 miles (115.3km) from Conca. 14.5 miles (23.3km) 8 hours from last hut (Mori); 6 miles (9.7km) 6 hours to next hut (Pietra-Piana). Approximately twenty-four sleeping places. Cold shower available.

Refuge De Pietra-Piana
Situated on a grassy terrace at the head of the Manganello Valley, below and to the south of Monte Rotondo. Altitude 6,043ft (1,842m) 43.7 miles (70.4km) from Calenzana; 65.6 miles (105.6km) from Conca. 6 miles (9.7km) 6 hours from last hut (Manganu); 6.5 miles (10.5km) 4.5 hours to next hut (L'Onda). Approximately twenty sleeping places. Small dining room. Mountain rescue service is based here with a helicopter landing area. There is an enclosure for camping.

Refuge De L'Onda
Situated below the north-west side of Monte d'Oro and adjoining the immediate east side of Bocca d'Oreccia. Altitude 4,692ft (1,430m) 50.2 miles (80.8km) from Calenzana; 59.1 miles (95.2km) from Conca. 6.5 miles (10.5km) 4.5 hours from last hut (Pietra-Piana); 6.3 miles (10.1km) 5.75 hours to Vizzavona. The last stage on the GR20 before Vizzavona. Approximately twenty sleeping places. Remote spot. Takes its name from the nearby bergerie.

Refuge De Capanelle
Situated just above the D169 roadhead branch between Chisoni and the Col de Verde, at the ski-tour station on the north-east side of Renoso. Altitude 5,381ft (1,640m). 65.1 miles (104.8km) from Calenzana; 44.2 miles (71.2km) from Conca. 8.6 miles (13.9km) 4.5 hours from Vizzavona; 7.3 miles (11.8km) 4 hours to next hut (Col de Verde). A small hut, approximately fifteen sleeping places. There is a restaurant nearby with opportunities to buy simple backpacking food supplies. A large car park. Taxi hire is possible.

Col De Verde
At the Col de Verde on the D169 road there is a private refuge made of wood. It belongs to the nearby bar/restaurant. Altitude 4,229ft (1,289m). 72.4 miles (116.6km) from Calenzana; 36.9 miles (59.4km) from Conca. 7.3 miles (11.8km) 4 hours from last hut (Capanelle); 2.3 miles (3.7km) 2 hours to next hut (Prati). A small refuge, approximately twelve sleeping places. Beware of the mice! The good bar/restaurant provides excellent hospitality.

Refuge De Prati
Situated south of the Col de Verde road pass. Altitude 5,971ft (1,820m). 74.7 miles (120.3km) from Calenzana; 34.6 miles (55.7km) from Conca 2.3 miles (3.7km) 2 hours from last hut (Col de Verde); 7.6 miles (12.2km) 5.5 hours to next hut (D'Usciolu). About twenty-four sleeping places.

Refuge 'Laparo' (off route)
Situated 10 minutes walk to the east of the GR20 on the path down to San Gavino. There is a water source a few minutes below the hut.

Refuge D'Usciolu
Situated at the southern end of the ridge about 7 miles south of the Prati hut. Altitude 5,741ft (1,750m) 82.3 miles (132.5km) from Calenzana; 27.0 miles (43.5km) from Conca. 7.6 miles (12.2km) 5.5 hours from last hut (Prati); 10.4 miles (16.7km) 8 hours to next hut (D'Asinao). Approximately fifteen places.

Refuge De Pedinelli
This is now a ruin which provides no shelter. The water here is polluted. There is a source 5 minutes higher on the GR route.

Refuge D'Asinao
Situated at the south-eastern foot of Incudine at the top of the Asinao Valley. Altitude 5,020ft (1,530m). 92.7 miles (149.2km) from Calenzana; 16.6 miles (26.7km) from Conca. 10.4 miles (16.7km) 8 hours from last hut (D'Usciolu); 9.3 miles (15.0km) 5.5 hours to next hut (Paliri). Approximately thirty places.

Refuge De Paliri
The most southerly hut in Corsica situated under the south-east face of the Tafonata di Paliri towers. Altitude 3,478ft (1,060m). 102.0 miles (164.2km) from Calenzana; 7.3 miles (11.8km) from Conca. 9.3 miles (15.0km) 5.5 hours from last hut (D'Asinao). Approximately twenty sleeping places. Water source can run dry after several weeks of drought.

APPENDIX 2   FACILITIES ON THE GR20

Camping
Wild camping is officially banned in the National Park. Camping is permissible in the following areas:-

(1) In the vicinity of the mountain huts, with the permission of the warden.

(2) In the neighbourhood of a bergerie, provided that the prior permission of the owner/guardian has been obtained. A fee (if any) is negotiable. Remember that these folk have a hard life and reasonable charges for camping and simple food will do much to supplement their income.

(3) At the official campsites at Calenzana, Bonifato, Conca and Sainte-Lucie de Porto Vecchio. Fees are payable.
Note that there is no official campsite in Vizzavona, but camping appears to be allowed unofficially on the grass at the side of the railway.

Hotels

Calvi	A wide choice of hotels.
Calenzana	(1) Bel Horizon. One star Tel: 62.71.72 Open only in the main season.
	(2) Monte Crosso. One star Tel: 62.70.15 Open all the year.
Haut Asco	Chalet du Haut Asco. One star Tel: 47.81.08 Open only in the main season.
Col de Vergio	Castel de Vergio. One star Tel: 48.00.01 Open all the year.
Vizzavona	(1) Hôtel Modern. The best of the hotels in the village. Excellent meals are available. The hotel also runs a refuge. There is a small grocer's shop in the hotel courtyard.
	(2) Hôtel de la Gare. This hotel has a restaurant but only dormitory facilities.
	(3) Beausejour Hôtel
	All these hotels are only open in the main season.
Conca	There are no hotels in Conca.
Porto Vecchio	A wide selection of hotels.

Apart from the above accommodation it may be possible in an emergency to find a room for the night at one of the bergeries, on or near to the route, but do not rely on this. Remember that these people have a hard working life and should not be pestered by ill-prepared walkers.

Food

Bar/Restaurants

Calenzana - There are several bars and restaurants in the town. The GR20 Restaurant can be recommended, serving traditional Corsican food.

Bonifato - There is a small restaurant at the L'Auberge de la Forêt.

Haut Asco - Meals can be obtained at the hotel (when open).

Col de Vergio - Good food and wine may be obtained at the hotel/restaurant 'Castel di Vergio'. This is a short diversion from the GR20.

Vizzavona - The hotels serve meals to non-residents. The dinner at the Hôtel Modern can be especially recommended. There is a café in the village.

Capenelle - There is a café/restaurant here, where simple meals may be purchased.

Col de Verde - There is an excellent bar/restaurant situated by the refuge. Good food and hospitality may be found here.

Col de Bavella - There are two cafés at this tourist attraction viz. 'L'Auberge du Col' and 'Le Refuge'.

Conca - Several cafés and restaurants are found in the town.

Grocer's Shops
Food suitable for backpacking may be bought in épiceries in the following places:-

Calenzana - Several shops with a wide selection.

Bonifato - A small store of supplies is usually kept at L'Auberge de la Forêt.

Haut Asco - Limited amounts of simple foodstuffs may be purchased at the hotel 'Le Chalet'.

Col de Vergio - The hotel 'Castel di Vergio' (a little off the route) keeps a small épicerie.

Vizzavona - There is a good épicerie in the yard of the Hôtel Modern.

Capenelle - The bar/restaurant has a small selection of lightweight and other foodstuffs.

Col de Bavella - A good grocer's and general-purpose shop may be found here.

Conca - Several foodshops are available.

Food may also be bought at the several villages, some distance from the route of the GR20. The only one that can be easily reached is Vivario, two stops on the train from Vizzavona, but it would only be necessary to make this excursion if the épicerie in Vizzavona was closed down. Other possibilities include Guagna during the Col de Vergio to Vizzavona section, Zicavo from the Col de Verde to Bavella section, and Zonza, 5.6 miles (9km) from the GR20 in the Col de Bavella region. All these detours entail a considerable amount of descent and re-ascent and a delay of at least a day. It may of course be necessary to go down to a village to replenish supplies if your party has been forced to encamp because of bad weather or illness. Otherwise to have to resort to these tiring detours would be a result of bad planning.

Note that food stores attached to hotels or bar/restaurants along the route, will normally only be open whilst the establishment itself is open. Most of them are closed outside the main season.

Snack Meals

It may be possible to buy snacks (such as bread and cheese or dried sausage) at the following bergieries:-

> Bergerie de Ballone (they have a calor gas fridge/freezer here; Day 3).
>
> Bergerie de Vaccaghia (Day 4).
>
> Bergerie de Tolla (Day 6).
>
> Bergerie d'Alzeta (Day 8).
>
> Bergerie de Palaghiolu (Day 11; 25 minutes walk from the GR20 in the region of the Ruisseau de Casimintello).

Several other bergeries may sell several simple snacks but only ask if there is a sign indicating the fact.

General Facilities

Postal, telephone and transport facilities on the GR20 are only to be found in Calenzana, Vizzavona and Conca. Simple gifts may be purchased in these villages, but a far better selection will be found in Calvi, Porto Vecchio, Ajaccio and Bastia.

APPENDIX 3   BIBLIOGRAPHY

1. *Corsican Mountains* by Robin G.Collomb (1982) West Col Productions.

2. *Classic Walks in France* by Robert Hunter and David Wickers (1985) Oxford Illustrated Press. This includes a chapter on the GR20.
3. *Classic Walks of the World* ed. Walt Unsworth (1985) Oxford Illustrated Press. This has an account of the Haute Corse section of the walk from Vizzavona to Calenzana.
4. *Granite Island* A portrait of Corsica by Dorothy Carrington (1984) Penguin Travel Library.
5. *Michael Green Guide to Corsica* Good general information on most tourist aspects of the island. Versions in English and French.
6. *Guide des Montagnes Corses Randonnées Pedestres et Escalades* (1985) Didier & Richard. In French.
7. *Gîtes d'étape de Randonnée et Refugees, France et Frontière* by Annick & Serge Mouraret, 4th ed. (1990). La Cadole lists some 3,300 establishments including all those in Corsica. In French with an English lexicon.

APPENDIX 4   USEFUL ADDRESSES

1. French Government Tourist Office, 178, Piccadilly, London WIV 0AL. Tel: (071) 493 3371.
2. Corsican Tourist Offices:-
    (i) L'Office du Tourisme, Syndicat d'Initiative, Hôtel-de-Ville, Place Foch, 20000 Ajaccio, Corsica. Tel: (95) 21.40.87.
    (ii) L'Office du Tourisme, Chemin de la Plage, 20260 Calvi, Corsica. Tel: (95) 65.05.87.
    (iii) Syndicats d'Initiative, 2 Rue du Marechal Juin, 20137 Porto-Vecchio, Corsica. Tel: (95) 70.09.58.
3. British Consulate, Hôtel des Estrangers, Ajaccio, Corsica. Tel: (95) 21.01.26.
4. Corsican National Park, L'Association du Parc, Natural Régional de la Corse, Boite Postale 417 - 20184 Ajaccio, Corsica.
5. Mountain Rescue Service in Corsica. Tel: Ajaccio (95) 22.37.02.

6. Falcon Holidays (Specialists in air travel to Corsica) 33 Notting Hill Gate, London W11 3JQ or Brazenose House, Brazenose Street, Manchester M2 5BH or 5 Royal Exchange Square, Glasgow G1.
7. Stanfords (Specialist Map Shop) 12-14 Long Acre, Covent Garden, London WC2E 9LP. Tel: (071) 836 1321.
8. The Map Shop, 15 High Street, Upton-upon-Severn, Worcestershire WR8 0HJ.

IF YOU LIKE ADVENTUROUS ACTIVITIES ON MOUNTAINS OR HILLS YOU WILL ENJOY READING:

CLIMBER
AND HILLWALKER
MOUNTAINEERING/HILLWALKING/TREKKING ROCK CLIMBING/SCRAMBLING IN BRITAIN AND ABROAD

AVAILABLE FROM NEWSAGENTS, OUTDOOR EQUIPMENT SHOPS, OR BY SUBSCRIPTION (6-12 MONTHS) FROM OUTRAM MAGAZINES, THE PLAZA TOWER, EAST KILBRIDE, GLASGOW G74 1LW

THE WALKERS' MAGAZINE

the great OUTDOORS

COMPULSIVE MONTHLY READING FOR ANYONE INTERESTED IN WALKING

AVAILABLE FROM NEWSAGENTS, OUTDOOR EQUIPMENT SHOPS, OR BY SUBSCRIPTION (6-12 MONTHS) FROM OUTRAM MAGAZINES, THE PLAZA TOWER, EAST KILBRIDE, GLASGOW G74 1LW

Printed in Gt. Britain by
CARNMOR PRINT & DESIGN
95-97 LONDON RD. PRESTON